FREUD'S GRAFFITI

for

Catherine
&
Dorothy Claris Kent

The
'Immortal Beloveds'

FREUD'S GRAFFITI

Collected Poems

1974–2024

Kevin Bailey

BY THE SAME AUTHOR:

By The Way, Collected Haiku (Red Moon Press, 2023)
Misericord (Dempsey & Windle, 2019)
Surviving Love (bluechrome publishing, 2007)
Prospero's Mantle (bluechrome publishing, 2006)
The Acorn Book of Contemporary Haiku [ed. with Lucien Stryk]
  (Acorn Book Co, 2000)
Poems and Translations (The Day Dream Press, 1987)

ACKNOWLEDGEMENTS:

Thanks to the editors of the following magazines and anthologies
in which some of these poems have appeared: *The Wallingford Mag-
azine, New Age, Civil Service Poetry* (EU), *Poetry Nippon* (Japan), *Kō
Magazine* (Japan), *Brussels Sprout* (US), *Envoi, Candelabrum, Cicada*
(Japan), *Odyssey, Ore, Critical Forum* (India), *Hummingbird* (US),
Iota, Kitap-lik (Turkey), *South, North West Literary Forum* (US), *Poetry
Cornwall, Outposts, Poetry Today* (India), *Staple, The Black Mountain
Review* (Ireland), *Modern Haiku* (US), *The Honest Ulsterman* (Ireland),
The Mainichi Daily News (Japan), *Orbis, The SHOp* (Ireland), *The
Frogmore Papers, Variations* (Switzerland), *Stand, Woodnotes* (US),
Acumen, Star Trek: The Poems (Iron Press), *Haiku for Lovers* (QMP),
Poetry on the Lake Journal (Italy).

My thanks also to Catherine Roberts for her careful proof-reading
and Mike Hogan for his friendly criticism and advice.

The cover design is taken from an etching by Catherine Roberts.

First published in 2025 by The Day Dream Press
in association with Stravaigers.

ISBN: 978-1-9164789-2-3

Printed & bound by Imprint Digital, Exeter
https://digital.imprint.co.uk

CONTENTS

A TREADING OF UNCERTAIN WAYS

ABROAD

SIX INTRODUCTORY NOTES
FOR THE READER

It is my own self that I am painting. Here drawn from life, you will read of my defects and my native form ... In the spirit of Montaigne, I offer these six short revelatory notes to the reader.

All the poems in this book are alchemical experiments: the mixing of poetic base elements to create my own poetic Philosopher's Stone ... A fantasy of course — a lifetime's fantasy of work with the aim of transforming common language into golden eloquence. If I had succeeded, I would have had a cure for my own personal suffering, a restoration of youth, and be endowed with immortality ... but the Adept never gives up hope: the investment in time and energy is too great. Every experiment, whether it succeeds or fails, is instructive. Thankfully, in this less exact science of poetry, 'succeed' or 'fail' relies on each reader's subjective judgement — that random mix of unique personal factors that keeps the appreciation of any poem in a state of flux; the poetic equivalent of Schrödinger's Cat ...

I started writing poetry in the late 1960s within the culture of Lawrencian 'free love', Women's Lib, Hippy excesses and an English poetry 'scene' which, at core, seemed totally unaffected or stimulated by the zeitgeist, and which by the late '70s had fallen back into an inward-looking post-Georgian blandness and the 'Gentility' defined by Alvarez. There were notable exceptions, but the English traditionalists in gown, town and countryside seemed to dominate ... I realize all this can be contradicted, but it was how I saw things then.

In 1971 Ezra Pound was still very much alive, and at seventeen I was ripe for conversion to a broader historical and cultural view of poetry: his *ABC of Reading* was the catalyst — from then on, my appreciation and understanding of poetry became pan-temporal and pan-cultural. My reading became a series of untidy chain-reactions: Sappho would lead to Seferis or Ritsos; The Provençal poets to Dante, Rossetti, Lorca, Celan; the Jewish poets of Spain to the ghazals of Ibn 'Arabi; and the T'ang poets of China to the haiku masters of Japan. The ability to travel from culture to culture, poet to poet across time and space by means of reading and imagination is euphoric — and powerfully addictive. It is a concoction I strongly recommend, and has energized whatever creativity I possess for over fifty years: I could not live without it. My poetry is made of it. As Arthur Symons says: 'The making of one's life into art is after all the first duty and privilege of every man. It is to escape from material reality into whatever form of ecstasy is our own form of spiritual existence.'

Love is a paradox. It has so many different forms of habit and expression that it can only really be understood at the personal level. The individual's experience of it will always be unique, and where my own poetic exploration of love is concerned, I can only echo the words of the Spanish poet Luis Cernuda: 'I have only tried, like every man, to find my truth, my own, which will not be better or worse than that of others, only different.' Truth is essential, and my own experience of love has evolved from a youthful phallo-centricity into a mature understanding of 'the other' and the equality of difference. It is said that love is a beast with two horns — passion and hatred; positive and negative. This is a dynamic in all relationships that plays out with either the mellowing victory of enduring love, or its fracturing defeat as a consequence of a multitude of incompatibilities. Sometimes the failure is more definitive: an act of betrayal or cruelty, however manifested. Both sexes are culpable ... If we are lucky, fate eventually puts us on that unmapped path that leads to 'the immortal beloved' — which is never an ideal, but a complex fusion of two individuals within one experience. As far as my own love poetry goes, I take comfort from the words of Edmond de Goncourt: 'Anyone who cannot feel passionate love — for women or flowers ... or wine — anyone who is not in some way unreasonable or unbalanced, will never never never have any talent for literature.'

Stendhal begins his autobiographical *Life of Henry Brulard* by describing the view of Rome he had from the Janiculum Hill: 'against my will ancient Rome prevailed over modern Rome; memories of Livy crowded into my mind ...' He was nearly fifty and musing on the inevitability of death and soberly reflecting: 'Why, greater men than I have died ... if there be another world, I shall not fail to go and see Montesquieu. If he says to me, *my poor friend, you never had any talent at all*, I should be sorry but not in the least surprised — who can see himself?'

All this came to mind recently when I was standing atop White Horse Hill in my native Berkshire. It was a hot summer's day: I didn't look east towards my birth town, but south-west. Few people realize that 'as the crow flies' there are no cities or large towns until that undistracted bird reaches Exeter, a hundred miles away. It is a land of chalk plains, ancient villages and monuments that pre-date Rome. It is a land apart, and we, proudly born within its bounds, call it Wessex ...

Man and boy, in all weathers I've stood on White Horse Hill and inhaled 'history': it's puffed me up with pride for a land that, in my imagination, connects not with a dull England north of the Thames but to a Romantic South: the old Angevin lands of Eleanor of Aquitaine; the Provence of the Troubadours; Islamic Al-Andalus; and the Mediterranean Empires of Rome and Greece. Walking the chalk-dusted paths of Wessex — over empty Plains and sensual Downs — my fantasies can transport themselves to any of these parallel lands.

This is why I've always thought of myself as an 'European', not an 'English' poet. But, who can see himself? Who can judge himself? Al Alvarez wrote to me once: 'You are a real lyric poet and that's not an easy thing to be these days. The love poems, especially the sequence Arthur & Amelie, are as good as any I've read in a long time — pure, translucent, economical, and erotic, an achievement to be proud of. Don't fret about whether or not some ignoramus reviews them, you've made them as perfect as you can, and that, in the end, is not only all that matters, it's also the only true satisfaction. History, fickle whore or not, will be your judge ...' But self-doubt and poetic self-reflection will find me standing beside Henri Beyle in the world beyond, likewise unsurprised to be branded talentless ...

Jacques Prévert, after completing the script for *Les Enfants du Paradis*, is reported to have said 'cinema and poetry are the same thing....' For me, this is true. Films have always stimulated my imagination, and many of my poems are just scenes or scenarios from unmade films. I am a frustrated film-maker, and have been dogged by a visual and dramatic Muse all my creative life. She is slightly louche, smokes, drinks and leans over my shoulder reeking of a seductive perfume that I'm certain I didn't buy her. She is a true femme fatale from any film noir you'd care to name. In human form she's Simone Simon in *La Bête Humaine* (and *Cat People*) — or Gloria Grahame in *The Big Heat*.... She can look after herself — and she has often deserted me — only to return, full of insincere promises on my darkest 'nights of the soul', her warm breath on my neck, reducing me to a stock Balzacian character set upon by The Succubus. I always allow her to guide my potentially deceived hand. Lang, Renoir, Prévert, Kubrick —

she's had amours with all of them. One day she will leave me ... Perhaps we'll meet again, in some dark Paradise. Reader; beware of her charms.

I have a flip side. Turn over the face of the Muse and there are the Janus heads of psychology and astronomy looking either way. Both observe objectively, but the astronomer is the purer and more reliable of the two. The psychologist has, too often, experienced life on both sides of that borderland between rationality and madness. Arthur Symons knew all about this: 'The artist, it cannot be too clearly understood, has no more part in society than a monk in domestic life: he cannot be judged by its rules, he can be neither praised nor blamed for his acceptance or rejection of its conventions. Social rules are made by normal people for normal people, and the artist is fundamentally abnormal.'

Anthony Storr has explored this creative 'abnormality' in *The Dynamics of Creation*, but reclassifies such abnormality as 'divine discontent'; 'the seeking of symbolic solutions to his [the artist's] problems in creative productions.' Which is rather more generous than Freud's blunt 'An artist is once more in rudiments an introvert, not far removed from neurosis. He is oppressed by excessively powerful instinctual needs. He desires to win honour, power, wealth, fame and the love of women; but he lacks the means for achieving these satisfactions. Consequently, like any other unsatisfied man, he turns away from reality and transfers all his interests, and his libido too, to the wishful constructions of his life of phantasy, whence the path might lead to neurosis ...'

I prefer to accept the judgement of Symons, rather than the analysis and classification of Freud. But both have a point, and Freudian introspection has lingered like a wraith through much of Western art during the last hundred years. The contents of this book are no different. My poems are an expression of my own id, ego and superego — hopefully free from 'ego-boundary sclerosis'. My poems were written for my own gratification, and to satisfy that mysterious need some of us have to share our thoughts and ideas creatively. These motivations have remained unchanged from the time humans first decorated cave walls with an outline of their hand. They are not the Freudian motivations of Eros or Thanatos (though each of these may be a factor) but simply (I would argue) a consequence of the desire to say: 'I was here. I created this.' I am no different. The poems I invite you to read in this book are an affirmation of my existence and a shout into the void. You are human, you will understand.

KB

ARTHUR & AMÉLIE

Eight Scenes from The Natural History of Love

Your head turns away: O the new love!
Your head turns back: O the new love!

—Rimbaud

for
Al Alvarez

SCENE I

A Solitary Boy

In the church, a solitary boy
practising *cantata* — his notes
                              skittering
among the old rafters. The dangling bell-pulls.
The oscillating ropes.
In the heavy air, a *Magdalena* has undressed.
Plaster white breasts
                    rubbing
through a chemise of dull blue paint.
She steps down from her plinth. Shakes
her hair. Gold flakes
                    in a shaft of light.
A voice, breaking.

SCENE 2

Amélie

The sea of waiting, like the breasts of Amélie
are sucked dry by the boy's imaginings;
   this little *Arthur*
                  who has no time —
out of the mind comes eternal life. Dark words
in a milk sea. The boat of paper; a *Hermes*
along the gutter, to the drain, to the sewer,
to the river — and on, to an ocean where only
Zeus as sun, and eyes beyond a mortal horizon
read.

SCENE 3

Man and Girl

In her black coat and green dress
she stands among the bluebells.
Sunlight still makes it through the trees.
A young smile. Hands in pockets.
Unable to resist him
                  the man's hands
draw out two white breasts, like eggs
stolen from a nest. They can be crushed.
It is a crime. He puts them back. Nipples
skiffle down the withdrawing knuckles.
She turns. He will be back. The path is set.
Twilight fades to black.

SCENE 4

Christian

The clematis has pushed a pale twine of leaf
through the old window frame. He notices this
as she holds his weighty scrotum like a bag of
gold coin. He is resigned. Calm, despite the theft
that she intends to make. He has no cloak or shirt
to give. No other things to heap upon her. Love
he can give. Forgiveness. The plant has lost its way.
Will cling to anything. Her fingers are climbing.
The grip tightening. The pleasure, moving.

SCENE 5

Epiphany

Her small narrow buttocks:
like an uncluttered boy, press upward.
Her breasts are smothering the white sheets.
Her hair is an exhausted blackbird
and her slim legs
                unicorns chained in flight.
Her anus is a purple star
                    and her cunt
the baby's eye, part awake
                      part in slumber —
puffed, not fully shut; reacting
to the sun's light;
               opening up
the wet epiphany that marks her life.

SCENE 6

A Well Known Stranger

All day alone. Glass, the sun, and an
unresponsive telephone
                          keeping her
convented within the almost sacred smell
of waxed furniture, and the frustrated
ritual of wandering upstairs
to the neatly made bed.
                        She opens a window.
In her breast a pain. The sound of bird song.
A desire to be naked and warm.
                            Time
passes. From a mirror, the chance glimpse
of a well known stranger.
                       Spring
arouses her, although nothing has changed.

SCENE 7

Eve

Marching on into you
                all the new men —
all the men of your dreams. The future highway.
The stars gleam in the water of your eyes.
The flesh yields like dough.
The plump rounding moon
                   is tethered inside.
You rise up. Somnambulist, out of the wifely bed.
Sweat glistens all over your body.
The conjugal seed seeps.
A disorderly queue of Herms await your pleasure.
Much will be new.
            You will savour it like honey.

SCENE 8

La Vita Nuova

A bee hovers over her nipple.
She does not move.
                        Her lover watches.
A spill of yellow pollen has rained down
under the beating wings. A small shadow
is targeting her heart.
                        The nipple swells
and slowly rises.
                        Around her hips, the rippled
blue dress is tight. She moves a little.
Breasts swim to find their own level
                                as she sits.
The bee has gone. She has made up her mind.
Cornflowers and poppies
                        catch her eye.
She has more now than the man can give.

WANDERER

I never understood quite what was meant by God.

—Edward Thomas

FOX

Exposing himself from the hedge,
the gargoyled face of a fox; panting
his shame; doing the quick-change
to guilty expressions of movement:
skipping off across shit-brown furrows,
satisfied with my shock; only a back-
ward glance at one who understands.

APOSTATE

Plainsong deep within the church:
stones and sound one. I can only
approach, outside, among the dead:
I cannot attune to this hymnal God.

Dry grasses rustle. The wild flowers;
Hard-head, Campion and *Chamomile*,
tap the hot, lichen-spat tombs.

I breathe freely. This is youth regained;
not in the old bones or flesh that carry
all this doubt, but in the loosened faith
and open air. I lay back and take it in.

'WALKING TOM'S GHOST

Chalk dust on her feet from the Downland path —
the perfect imprints, left by cornflowers,
blue as the sky; blue as her eyes, that look away
from the nearby sounds of harvesting.

How far ahead she always walks — brown legs
and slender hips leading the beast.
The first autumn rain will erase her steps:
her shadow, grown long into the past.

AT EASTBURY, BERKSHIRE

for Helen Thomas

Scattered
through the mourning heads of barley,
the poppies' death rattle;
while overhead,
the skylark and higher kestrel
are cut to shape by October gales ...

Up here,
the first touch of Autumn rain —
West-blown, chills my face;
the kiss of many souls,
drifting, over khaki-coloured fields,
hunting out each lost embrace ...

GRANDPA, 1961

That old bubble of an Austin 35 —
Grandpa, crackly
in his grey trench coat,
draws
through his smart ciggy holder
a tang of Turkish smoke
that glows
with deepened thought
in the cloudy twilight ...

We turn for home:
gravity's swing —
the bright
orange indicator
snaps out —
the warm leather seats grip:
I look across —
the silence of 1918
still cast upon his brow.

CORN FIELD

The fly-flecked Moon,
tatter grey,
plugs the stretched blue
summer sky
        tight:

A nipple of white
on the night-side breast
of embracing God.

Listen.
There are tunes
of unbound love
in the rustling twilight ...

YERMA

Gathering the scent of almond blossom
on this still, moonlit, March night;
I remember you, and the slight curve
of your flank, and the fresh smell
of white flesh pressed by my weight —
in a depth of sheets met, this odour
of love made then — and here, a breeze
risen ghost; the affect of cursed body
and sense, that knows itself, yet aches:
growing satiate — but incomplete.

WASP

A dead wasp
clings to my copy
of Baudelaire.

How appropriate
that this vicious,
foetal thing

should expire
on these
sickly flowers.

STORM & STILL BIRTH

A chaos of clouds scudding through dark eyes.
The hand's descent from forehead, and down
crossing breasts — her triangulation of faith —
fingers lingering to gather sense from the storm-
coloured nipples. Silently, it thunders in her heart.

So plain the emptiness of these human hands —
their miming shape around this loss: the empty,
emptying gesture. Acid tears trickle out, fall
and glisten in the lightning's shock, burning
like the jilted child that's slipped her womb —

this nameless lump, damned by some lesser god.
The bruised sky rages, blindly, in our thoughts.

FISH

Fish, still in water
clear as ice,
holding pace
with the flowing force.

I know its cold ways
and sideways stare:
the cold pulses
rushing over eyes —

its fixed tranquillity,
hiding its still rage
at passing time —
and nature's futility.

HARE

I found the severed
head of a hare
staring a dry stare

and gobbing flies
in the long grass
by the river.

The passing shiver
of charnel *Nature*
closing tired eyes.

INTO THE DARK GARDEN

My breath, foul with the taste of tobacco smoke
never made her flinch, as sometimes, in my anger,
I'd wound her with a putrid kiss ... And as she smiled,
I'd drive myself away into the dark garden, finding,
in the scent of herbs, her spell, homing me back
to where she stood, rocking her hips, bright in the
old doorway, caressing with words and a gentle touch
the black beast whose mask had slipped ...
This wasn't modern love, but something older —
binding by blind instinct the rough to the smooth.
And now she's gone, I cannot be harmed by this
colder world — her irritating warmth burns within.

ON THE ROAD

I cycled along the damp road: the winnowed
hedges, gates, and stagnant ditches of fleet
interest to one so absorbed in the mechanical
task of turning pedals faster and faster ...

It is a calming thing, this going nowhere.
Only the wind has produced tears that count —
the dusk is close but unreachable. There has
been a death to deny. My heart pumps ...

In the dark, light-less, I have arrived by
chance at somewhere that confronts her ghost.
The moon — old friend — boldly rises over a
naked landscape: is it *now* I'll accept her loss?

TURNING THE CORNER

I turned the corner. This is a phrase
with other meanings.

I got well. I got solvent.
I improved my view of life.

I turned the corner —
brick wall giving way to street?

Tall hedge to bucolic avenue?
I turned the corner, and saw the road

so many have imagined:
the described ways

I have seen as a fellow traveller:
the clichéd *journeys of the mind*

visualised at every turn, however
unexpected, yet still familiar.

POEM ON HER BIRTHDAY

i.m. Dorothy Claris Kent

i

'*Sweet Thames*' — not so sweet in Winter
when your blackness is a flood and you
become the Styx I cross to the grave of
one I loved *above all others* — hard dug into
her flinty snug, close by the church that
made sparse punctuation in her life,
of love and labour — and few rewards ...

ii

'*Sweet Thames*' — is true in Summer, when
I cross; bright bouquet held to my heart,
gathered from fields in which she played —
her memories waving as I pass, carried
to that soft mound under which she lay,
comfortable at last — a Godly rest, for one
denied her living worth: my debt; *still unpaid*.

WANDERER

This aimless drift through a landscape
down lanes
urban and rural
in the fall of the year
feet scuffing
making a wake through the duns and reds

the step varied
sometimes breaking into a healing stride
to out-pace the dogged moods
that chased behind.

Long ago
there were familiar hearths to target
when the mind was dulled
and the long walk to grandmother
lover or wife gave equal sanctuary —
but it is gone.

Those doors are strangers
and the autumn leaves
no longer burn my feet
in expectation.

Out in the damp twilight
I have become my own myth,
the season's wanderer
never finding sanctuary
until love
and home find me.

INSOMNIA

In the dark,
clouded by this quiet
in which a solitary bird sings
and a cat purrs
romancing
on its lover's bed,
the pitch-thick air
snuffs out
the dreamer's lies.

All peace
on this dust-speck's
sun-less side
is un-consecrated.
God falls
through the neck
of an hour-glass.
Dawn; *une horloge qui ne sonne pas —*
a clock that never strikes...

CLOCK

Dead clock — I am the shadow
that winds the spring and sets
the dial — that V-shaped smile
that gets you right: *tick-tock*.

Alive again, the petted time
fed with tension, and the
smooth rotation of jagged
brass, hidden, like our own

tick-tock. Don't stop, only
companion — the dark is a
better place when you talk.
What did you say? Ah, *tick-*

CARING

I think it was then I stopped caring —
children, lovers, mother; the immediate
light trivia, and more remote sense of
heavy responsibility that no one had
asked me to endure or bear: but old
and fearful — of sickness and death,
and all the accumulated failure,
I stopped caring — and there was
a kind of chilled peace that would
not last, but got me through today —
and past all those unfruitful yesterdays.

OUTSIDE

Outside
a foot-fall
on the pavement

some high
heeled laughter
and a silence —

a kiss?
The pushing desire
to know ...

We must resolve
not to be
confronted by
realities —

to confuse
our story

to allow
those strangers in
who would romanticize
our world.

FREUD'S GRAFFITI

From error to error, one discovers the entire truth.

—Sigmund Freud

for

H.

FREUD'S GRAFFITI

epic poem :

lost

at sea

nature poem :

green

as grass

war poem :

grave

men

sex poem :

moist

parts

love poem :

warm

embrace

last poem :

God

revealed

THE BATH

Louise has filled the white enamel bath ...
On a cork-topped stool, a brown paper-
bag of little oranges tears open: the floor
is scattered with setting suns. Her clothes
have crumpled onto a chair ... Salmon
pink shift; yellow cardigan; stockings;
a plain pair of briefs; a cotton brassière.
She pours blue oil from a jar. Sinks into
Aegean warmth; breasts, *Olympian* above
the foam. She leans forward; sleek shoulders —
a seagull cutting the air. From the depths,
a slick of red aborts her *Labyrinthine* tale.

ROSE HIPS

Rose hips
swollen red amphora

made of things
greener
than God's fingers

jostling for sun
in a swell of
noon wind

spread from the wreck
of a greying oak.

PIROUETTE

Pirouette. A lovely *turning* word.
Good on the mouth and tongue.
A pleasure of a r t i c u l a t i o n ...

The tutu-ed dancers in white:
their slender legs teetering
on the edge of collapse ...

The khaki body spinning round
spread by that *raping* velocity
as the bullets hit ...

The arts of life and death — like these
contrasting pirouettes, stilled by the
darkening stage, or receiving earth.

LA MAJA DESNUDA

Maria, Duchess of Alba by Francisco Goya

The *Nude Maja*, two hundred years old, pouts
from a postcard pinned to my work-shed wall —
still voluptuous, and saying 'Yes' to the unlocking
of her tight-pressed thighs, and the private chunk
of quim Señor Goya (against convention) splashed on
with a virile mix of linseed oil and red-hot umber ...

Such a neat seduction: her breasts spread so wide
they canvas to all mankind: 'Come, enjoy this place our
artist filled ...' Which suggests, not her easy flesh,
but the arid space within them both: the absence
of a constant heart becomes their mutual sin ...
'*Ergo te absolvo*', for heaven knows, I understand.

PORTRAIT OF SARAH

(In Autumnal Pallet)

By the fire-place; the fire, and a glow
on your face, breasts bronze at their
tapered ends and your long copper
hair thrown like a cowl over square
shoulders. You sit, prim as a cat,
naked, on your knees, on the mat;
the glint in your eyes, the straightness
of your back; pressed haunches, all
an overflow of sculpted flesh softened
in chiaroscuro. The books on every shelf
dancing; the walls, like Troy, golden.

CRIME SCENE

A frosty night. The stars
ferocious entry wounds of light
as God goes mad, stabbing
into every naked heart
their chill wonder.

I hear the omnipotent cry
of pain and frustration ...
Beyond the crystal spheres,
the babbling —
the booming remonstrations of regret.

WORK

Up.
Work.
Rain & lightbulbs.
New girl. Sexy. Backside. Glum day. Fantasies...
Cough. Splutter: *natter, natter, natter*. Dead minds.
FOR GOD'S SAKE STOP COUGHING! Cough:
natter natter. Cough. Go to sleep. Dream.
Sexy bouncy wiggle pink blond young but
crafty with her pale lips.
She. The other. Bouncy warm. Big breasted: OO
Kind hearted. Hard. Killed a spider. Only small,
smeared across the grey desk top.
So sad, bad luck. How to enter the warm stickiness
of a wiggle wiggle. Mentally.
People are so strange.

LILITH

*I saw the ardent face of the Succubus who laughed and addressed to me
a thousand exciting words ... Hearing which, under the prick of this tongue
which sucked out my soul, I plunged and precipitated myself
finally into Hell without finding bottom.*

—Honoré de Balzac [*Droll Stories*]

LILITH

her door is always ajar

offering

from the dark interior

something forbidden

something too sore

for the heart to bear

something unclean

we dare not enjoy

all monstrosity

is there

her door opens to misery

her hair strangles

with amorous cruelties

and yet we go in

devoted and mutable

the anointed sinner

SEX

With her open legs
she offers up
the shrimp-pink
aqueous
hole

A little worn perhaps
but honest
in its shawl
of matted
hair

*

I intrude,
parting lips
so much sweeter
than are often
kissed

And beyond
licentious flesh
the echo of myself
lives
on

.

.

.

BACK

I felt down her spine
with my fingers —

the knobs of bone
hard in the flesh;

primitive, part reptile,
part fish,

landed up,
and turned into this

in-curved shape,
flexing, bent

to take the hip-
locked weight

of my *Push* ...
Push ... *Push* ...

TANGLED ROOTS

Delicately pink as a baby's mouth
that's satiated with milk, a dribble
of sperm leaks out — a gentle flow —
the uterus pulsing back what it
does not need: the surplus gob
making more wet the stained bed;
this sexual canvas, bare as our flesh.

Our tangled bodies have pulled up
their tangled roots — we have quenched
them with tales of coital randomness
and past loves: we have brothers and
sisters-in-sex; an incest of memories
to bless this afternoon of sweat. We are
part of the *great flood*. We are *not* jealous.

HAIRS

I have hairs under the foreskin —
dark, trapped hairs, there, under
the foreskin. My little *pluckings*
from her, pulling at the skin like
wire cutting cheese, as she lay,
dead *plucked*, and recently plucking
from me, the intangible benefits
of orgasm and seed. Taken into her,
this short endurance merchandise:
and yet, here I have her hair; lasting
for a thousand years hair, trapped
under my cell-dying foreskin:
pieces of an ignored *immortality*,
privately stored, for this last reference.

CALIBAN

i

A year later, at the end of another wet August
and frequent meetings in strange places
she came back, body full to bursting
and spread naked on my bed, coveting
more of the same sweat and semen
that had brought all this change into our lives.

ii

Under her belly the child elbowed a plastic
wave across her flesh. His stumpy art pickled
in aspic. The mutated truth of this deceived life
made *sub rosa* for her husband's sake. I baptised
my son; and she transformed that perfect boy
into a lie's Caliban I cannot hope to mend.

UP THE GARDEN PATH

i

At the end of the garden
she showed me the night-scented stocks,
proud that such a sweet scent   .
could be absorbed
into the myth of our rank infidelity.

ii

Back in the house, her husband
washed the dirty crocks,
then bathed our kids ...
Such bourgeois gratifications,
such candy-covered lives.

AFFAIR

i

on a bench

two bodies defined by plastic flesh

pressed inward and outward —

here is a black feather

we can talk about ...

it is tempting

to touch your cheek —

scar it

with this invisible line of blackness —

your masochistic treat

ii

the oak enjoys the rough hair

above your hollow

the ground biting your flesh

the joy-filled pain

from scattered acorns —

from the green seed

entering

and nipples calloused

by the wind

uncapped and bitten

iii

and again

we gallop limbs

against brick walls

and taut springs

breaking distant bonds

the end of days

passion

that opened doors

of mourning

and shambled births

PURPLE LIPS

i

I rise to meet her:
almost gone within dark clouds
the scarlet sunset.

ii

Coal black the piled mat
of hair; here in my hand, and
there, padding my way.

iii

The purple lips
of my black-haired cat suck gently
on a little mouse.

THE AMULET

The necklace always made me hate her.
The slave chain: the conscience anchor
of fidelity ... Even when we fucked, this
spousal gift hung about her neck, flexing
its little links at every ecstatic breath.

It was her amulet; protecting husband
(home and wealth) ... He kept her fast;
and she cleaved, and every child we made
was taken for his own. Her body was his
church, and her belly — the sacred dome

under which such heresies of love and truth
were preached ... Even now, that golden
crucifix hangs between her sagging breasts:
Christ crucified, between two faithless rogues.

LAID OUT

You flatten on the neat bed:
breasts with all the sex let out —
belly, hips and pubic scribble
neutered in a lazy horizontal;
legs and hair gone *Dali-esque*.

Face; dead as a Greek mask.
What mood creates this laid-
out pose? The closed space;
a theatre of mute speculation
on this failed Lady Lazarus.

THE CRACKED MUG

The cracked mug
used for so long
now has deep brown veins
where once
there was a pure
and unbroken glaze.

Do I love the mug more
or less
for this varicose familiarity?
These common flaws
that shock my tongue
and scour my lips.

AMÉLIE

from the womb

she walks

through a night of blood

greedily

into a Lenten world –

our sweet vampire

Amélie

hounding

from your breasts

only crippled truths

TERMINUS

pulsating
the trains
from heart
to heartbeat

pausing
by
junctions

meetings

and love
murmurings
at stations

arriving
inevitably
at the end
of the line

TITANIC

In the cup
this half sunk
tea-bag,
the Titanic
of our love,
as we sit
in the cafe,
knowing
our talk
has become small
and our feelings
withered;
and yet,
still unsure
of how to say
good-bye.

POSTCARDS

Postcards: the ink of forty years ago fading.
Their concise entreaties to — '*Never go away*'
or '*stop loving*' now a patchy script, once
so familiar — and in their way, entrapping ...

That's unfair: an untruth — with hindsight,
more '*Entrancing*' ... Tickets to our erotic
madness — a mutual insanity that seemed
a force of nature when our bodies met ...

Forty years: the length of a short ice age,
and despite my heart's iciness, when our
child says: *Je tiens à toi* — it's her cards now
that enflame a more enduring kind of love ...

REMEMBRANCE

Crows are shouting *dead, dead.*

Trees. A lead sky.

It's colder than before —

the wind, rummaging undergrowth

like a wild beast.

Twenty years since we fucked

in this same damp place:

the madness upon us;

the tight cold flesh.

The graveyard is full of lovers.

I did not mean this living tomb —

this chill remembrance.

My words, you said, would be our curse.

Here, still crowing *dead, dead* ...

THERE IS A FINE PEAR TREE IN MY GARDEN*

I can't make sense of *things* anymore. The internal
flaws have shown themselves. There is a drought.
No tears have fallen for months. I have the odd
sympathy. Some *Bach* or *Beethoven* suggests what
I *might* feel, if I had the heart for it. A poetic ennui,
said unpoetically. *Dis*-integration is coming. *Crack!*
The beam above Jason's head — the curse of witches.
The cunts we take to bed — and make mothers of.
Children smothered in the womb. The father abjured.
Once, despite the uncertain bond, a son could fall
with tearful eyes upon his father's neck, for pride or
pity's sake. It's all Greek to me. Why *do* mothers fuck
their sons? And yet, I hold together for better times.
There is a fine pear tree in my garden. I live in hope.

* *Now when the steadfast goodly Odysseus saw his father thus wasted with age
and in great grief of heart, he stood still beneath a tall pear tree and let fall a tear.
[...] And sprang towards him, and clasped him in his arms, and kissed him,
saying: 'Lo, father, here before thee, my very self— cease from grief and tearful
lamenting [...]'*
                   —Homer: *The Odyssey*, Book XXIV

LE BOEUF SUR LE TOIT

or

The Ten Tragedies of Modernism

*The real resistance now is to an art which forces its audience
to recognize and accept imaginatively, in their nerve ends,
not the facts of life but the facts of death and violence:
absurd, random, gratuitous, unjustified, and inescapably
part of the society we have created.*

—Al Alvarez

for

D. M. Thomas & Mike Hogan

THE CAST OF CHARACTERS:

Le Boeuf sur le Toit (The Ox on the Roof)	A Parisian Cabaret and Bar
The Cacodylic Eye (L'Oeil Cacodylate)	A Painting by Francis Picabia
Ernest Hemingway	A Writer
Ezra Pound	A Poet
T. S. Eliot	A Poet
Marthe	Heroine of *The Devil in the Flesh*
Raymond Radguet	A Young Novelist
Jean Cocteau	Poet & Film Maker
Harlequin	A Clown
Columbine	A Clown's Mistress
Kurt Weill	A Composer & Lyricist
Drancy	A Paris Concentration Camp
Max Jacob	A Jewish Poet
Marianne Oswald	A Jewish Singer
Pierrot	A Clown & Rejected Lover of Columbine
Pablo Picasso	A Painter
Josephine Baker	An Afro-American Dancer & Resistance Fighter
Wyndham Lewis	A Right-Wing Artist
Francois Villon	A Medieval French Poet
Abraham Lincoln	An United States President
Ernst Von Rath	A German Diplomat
Herschel Gryszpan	Ernest's Jewish Lover & Assassin

ACT ONE

The sore *Cyclops* eye, scrawled with graffiti
is pulsing ... Some guys Jazz —

it's all *faire un boeuf*, as they say now;
and pressed up close to half-lit faces,
with swinging breasts and fleshy arses,
the girls are dancing, loud and hard —

Glasses rattle above the bar:

Ernest shouts to Ezra —

He should strangle his wife ... rob the bank
and bugger his psychiatrist ... Old Tom...

Cat lover ... Never fucked ... A sterile life ...
a Waste Land buddy ... true enough ...

ACT TWO

'You are Marthe, you are Marthe — Oh the erection
is music in your flesh Raymond ...

Hear me, hear me — come behind this velvet screen.
A kiss a kiss, My Pretty Boy ...'
Crazy Jean. Cocky Cocteau — *très sûr de soi.*

I have put my slim body by him. We have jerked.
The words flow. But, not *très sûr de soi* – no.

And the girls dance, and the tits swing
and in the half-light, back-stage
the white communion dress of my arse is ripped.

'Roses have only one season –
but you shall remain, *jeunesse dorée ...*'

'Devil – fuck you and die ...'

'*Être banal ... être banal ...*' you say.

You witch, you bugger — to twist my curse —
I should have had a happier life ...

ACT THREE

I have taken off my Harlequinesque —
my diamonds of green and red
too sharp for the dance of a gay gendarme
prancing the bar
all high-headed and boastful
about to arrest
petite Columbine
roughly trans-dressed
with a randy dwarf stuffed in her pants —

but *quelle horreur*! — my head,
guillotined by fresh air ... Ernest has laughed,
and takes a mock bet — the head is restored!
And all clown about in a humourless jig:

and a Devil takes shape
as the music plays on ...

ACT FOUR

Dawn —

Mistah Hemingway — he *not* dead.
The sun has risen over foggy *Oświęcim.*

Paris glows in the light. There's time yet ...

The carnivorous ape
has stopped playing with its mincing machine
for now —

and the crowds
are singing a Kurt Weill dirge,

and fear —
in the fractured minds of those who know,
know hedonism is the antidote to Hell ...

(*Oświęcim in Polish ... or Auschwitz in German*)

ACT FIVE

If black
ain't the colour of sadness, then here's Pierrot
in perfect white, and Pablo

tickling the girls to death
just waiting to tie them up in brushstrokes
that bend them into orgiastic curves

and eyes — always the eyes ... that state:
Pierrot never got his Columbine.

ACT SIX

It's a short taxi ride
to Drancy ...

Wyndham — amused,
stares with the long dead eyes
of an unsuccessful rapist ...
The day has come.

ACT SEVEN

The day has come.

Max and Marianne are giggling over a glass.
The sun is warm and crowds pass
the tables scattered in the boulevard
where couples multiply and chat …

Why not hit the Jew-girl in the face? Ernest —
put her in her place — this plain-faced kike
and the pansy with the pale visage …

Gentile or Jew, it doesn't matter
you'll insult them both,
until you blow your head off —
boom — and blast … You savage fuck.

Monsieur Jacob took the ride.
Marianne got the message, but wouldn't hide —
and Josephine threw the bananas back.

ACT EIGHT

From the Shades
the ghosts may chorus '*Wrong, wrong...*
I've always been wrong ...'

But nothing's changed — it's just the meek,
casting off their velvet chains,
who've grabbed us by the balls ...

We haven't gone away —

We are in the shade,
and see more clearly now;
Rome ne fu pas faite toute en un jour
as Villon sang —

Vide ... While old Abe
fondles the heads of the sweet *Fasci* ...

The lips and eyes cannot lie —
and there is no truce among the Gods;
but I say: there is love beyond all vanity ...

ACT NINE

Dusk ...

Night drifts into *Le Boeuf.*

The *Cyclops* eye blinds the empty stage
and the table-lights recede
ghosting in chiaroscuro the last
to fall into *Dante*'s blackness.

All fades ...

The hero's strut — the fool's parade:
all that remains is an echoing cast
of banal *Pierrots* – and *Columbine*,
sobbing in the dark ...

ACT TEN

The night has come.

Ernst has lit Herschel's cigarette —
they drink ... they go to bed ...
and the erotic bullet in the head
has ricocheted as Kristallnacht ...

And the ape grinds again:
Meat, Bones, Brains —
and forever, the sour tunes
that never change ...

REVOLUTION

Man is free, but his freedom ceases when he has no faith in it.

—Francesco Petrarca

for

Ann C.

ARIEL [WHISPERING] SPEAKS ...

... Weird creatures of four limbs
(two that walk and two that sin):
their heads, their flesh, their mutable
sacks of weight and shape ... their

strange parts that dangle and protrude
... boast embellishments and growths
or tunnel away into shambling interiors
... God's innocents: this *Humanity* —

how roundly you are stripped bare:
exposed as the cunt-work of Sycorax —
all Calibans, fouling this island Earth;
unredeemed by magic, books, or love.

REVOLUTION

Don't speak. Don't speak.
The man in the little room
is listening. Ears plugged,
listening to every word.

Don't move. Don't move.
The man in the little room
has eyes glued. Is watching,
watching every move.

Think, but do not speak.
Think, but do not move.
Think of the man in the
little room, thinking.

They cannot steal your
dreams. Speak and move
there. Until the man in
the little room sleeps.

Now, speak and move.
Kill the man in the little
room. Then, listen and
watch. Listen and watch.

'SUPERMAN' TRIPTYCH

Superman (Adolf)

Over the high mountains | over wood-framed houses
and Gothic cities | following tram lines
the shadow of wings | and *that man*
in chiaroscuro | smiling
waving | at the window
below | racing ground
and little people | waving back
mouthing | to strains of
Strauss | and Wagner
Oh Superman | *we love you so ...*

Superman II (Edvard)

Somewhere else | Oslo perhaps
by his bed | thin and frail

Edvard Munch | has caught a chill

and stares | and stares

his canvas | half to death
reflecting | what it means
to paint | unloved.

Superman III (Ezra)

Perhaps Pound | was right
about Usury | and all that stuff
re. *Commerce* | and the *Unenlightened*
fucking up | the artist's life.

MAN WITH A MOVIE CAMERA*

Odessa, 1929

The empty seats in the Kinema — velvet, row
after row of grey, falling as one rolling wave.
The film is silent on its tracks — cars and trams
glide past shops with Cyrillic signs: the carousel
is unwrapped and turns pretty girls up and down:
the crowd spin: fly-wheels, pistons, and springs
are true to their natural motions — each a slave,
sculpted to enslave — steel never looking better
than in its black and white costume ...

This comforting testament where even mono-
chrome smoke and grime, vagrants, empty parks
and the poor in lines, are beautiful. Behind this
revolution, this mute change, a music so loud
that it cannot break the silence of the clicking film.

*A silent film by Dziga Vertov with live music performed by
The Michael Nyman Band at St. George's Hall, Bristol on
26 September, 2003.*

THE TESTAMENT OF DR. MABUSE*

Dr. Mabuse's hypnotic gaze
has converted me to the *Dominion of Crime*.
Anarchy is the only way forward:
our demonic genius must pull
with the tide of Capitalist civilization.

It is a black and white argument:
Evil has all the best lines.
The private crucifixions of the few,
time and again, prove the futility of goodness ...
Embrace the criminal philosophy:

it is the mien of all we know.
Do not fight the true nature of Humanity:
go with the flow, and destroy,
as circumstances, and your abilities allow ...
The Universe will thank you for it.

Fritz Lang, 1932

ARTAUD'S CELL — 1937–1946

Who am I? Where do I come from? I am Antonin Artaud:
A new body will be assembled in which you will never again
be able to forget me.

An incoherent calligraphy — smearing shit
over walls: the insane man's Japanese scroll.

This cell is creative: it's my dumb scream —
'Not mad, but going mad ...'

...Combing my blood-stiffened hair —
normal: cutting my blood-stiffened hair —

normal: the World, normal ... Madness,
normal ... If I am mad, then set me free

to be mad in a world of the mad ...
(Before doctors there was no madness).

The cell walls are a manuscript, pardoning
this *Self* of the World's shit ...

The *free* are dying from this World madness.
My brothers and sisters are dying ...

And yet I believe in a sane Resurrection beyond
this *Hell* ... Deliver me whole, *Dear* Christ ...

DON'T READ THIS...

*The art of popular success lies simply in never putting
more on any one page than the most ordinary reader can
lick off it in his normally rapid, half-attentive skim over.*

—Ezra Pound

What are you doing? Why are you reading this?
Do you expect some revelation? A confession?
The hopeful reassurance that you do not sin alone?

I lead you on. You are drawn, willingly, to your
own destruction. You kneel before me with your
candle of acquiescence. Your hands shake.

The Rite begins ... What? A look of surprise when
the sacred blade of Words rips through your guts?
Is it too much, this pain of reading? Forgive me.

You are a blood-offering to sweeten the lips of my
psychotic Muse. It is She who craves this sacrifice
of an artless fool: I cast you back into the darkness.

This is the end of our random meeting. I abandon
you to your fate. Your shocked hatred means nothing
to me. Your insipid pleas are useless. You are gone.

NOAH

Nothing but rain
filling butts and gutters —
and a marooned cat
crying for relief.

The night patters
to its wet dawn.

At last,
I can fall asleep,
freed from dreams
of the world's end.

A TREADING OF UNCERTAIN WAYS

The lunatic, the lover and the poet
Are of imagination all compact

—Shakespeare [*A Midsummer Night's Dream*]

It only needs a very small quantity of hope to beget love.

—Stendhal

for
Catherine

A TREADING OF UNCERTAIN WAYS

In the sharp pine-wood she stands among
the slender trunks. His books are dented
with rain-drops. Should he rise and follow
her, or gather words? (*This has always
been his dilemma.*) Between two loves ...
Now lost in the dark wood; no hewing out
with axes from this delicate place. Night
falls. The stars cannot guide him through
this unnatural maze. His love, the search
for lost paths: a treading of uncertain ways.

COUNTING THE CLOUDS

On the red pullover
her lover
is heaping primroses

that avalanche away
from her little
but loving breasts;

rising and falling,
rising and falling
with each silent breath.

Across a universe
her steady green eyes
are counting the clouds.

RED MOON

A red moon swims
in the wine glass.

The day has been hot.

Drink *honeysuckle* and
the female scent of stocks.

Lead my feet blind

over the trampled grass
to your *earthy* lair.

Love me.

The night has a fearless air,
and the future,

a touching of white flesh.

POMEGRANATE

She was just so ripe — there is no other
word to describe this fullness of flesh,
breasts, thighs; round face, and bright
eyes — she was just so ripe, and ready
to burst like the pomegranate, held up,
eclipsing the sun: its light, a trans-
lucent pink — as she is naked ... I bite:
seeds and juice from this little fruit
on my lips, and, as always, afterwards.

THE SCENT

He strokes his beard in the crowded street
and is not surprised when from his hand
comes the talisman of one bitter scent:

tested on his tongue, it seems a blend
of lad's love with lavender, his fingers
and clumsy thumb have taken up:

an indistinct flavour, recalling her cries;
loud as a birth — and now the dilute
of a love he touched, that will not fade.

THE DOLL

Why the mask? This pale carnival mask —
fixed smile on ruby lips; black wig of
Greek curls; the doll's body too fragile
to handle ...

I will play with these limp arms and legs
until their sinews snap — twist the head
into every angle that is inhuman —
drop you,

just to hear the baked china crack —
dead eyes fanning the lashes to a fixed
stop .... And then, with a kind of regret,
I will try to mend

the broken parts; and in the process,
learn all I can of the doll-maker's art.

BATH TIME

In this warm bath
shared with hairy
Agamemnon
and loquacious
Marat
I try to ignore
my vengeful wife
rattling cutlery.

MY LIBRARY OF LIFE

My wife, *ma femme*, my library of life:
my books as flesh and flesh as books,
nesting, unalphabeticized, relating only
part to part, subject to subject, a creature
alive; the whole story in parts, whole, part
of the story of stories and on, *ad infinitum,*
from woman to woman, library to library
remoulded again and again; the old and
new; informing, the immortal beloved.

QUESTIONS

The old Georgian window, its evening lights
pastured into squares, and at its edge, your
naked frame, enclosed ... This pondering

of the shadows and twilight-haunts before
you'll come to bed, perturbs me. The pause:
a looking out for better things? A latent fear?

What is it? This question delays everything.
You come, reluctantly, to the warm sheets.
        Is it *now*, you will explain?

THE BLACK AND GREEN DRESS

I asked her (she was reluctant) to put on
the dress for remembrance of younger days.
She put on the dress. A faded black and green
pattern on Indian cloth. A tie at the back,
tightened, that draws the hem to mid-calf
and pulls the waist into a hand's dream —
and the breasts, as they should be, softened.
You wear the dress: nothing, but the dress —
bare feet and arms. Underneath, white flesh.
Only the dress has aged. Time, has always
seemed an irrelevance. Old decoration over
skin, over something, hidden, that is more.

PASTORAL

At the wood's edge,
wild flowers strangled
by the wind:

and among them,
your face, smiling
like a child.

The sun's not quite
in the stream.

Snaking over sandy
fish deserts

the dapple-green
water weeds ...

The boys
are bathing naked.

On your timid breast
this pink rose.

COPSE

The bluebells are dying back —
going out of focus under a fresh
leaf haze. In the copse, her small
white breasts glow in half naked-
ness: only pale wind-flowers and
red campion rise in competition.

Her dark hair sweeps shadows
through this old woodland space,
and dew clear, her green eyes reflect
bent branches, elongated clouds,
and a deeper sky than I can see ...

Our love has wandered far —
a silent hiatus to gather breath.

WET SUNDAY

A wet Sunday in May:
cascades of rain shower new leaves;
early roses bow their heads.

You have not dressed — in childhood
it would have been an afternoon of play:
the lost world of toys and books.

You lean forward from the couch
to grab the colour supplements —
paper rustles into shape.

From your dressing-gown
a breast casually escapes.
I am drawn to its softness and flow.

A Zen-like movement ...
It is frog weather: fish weather.
Your breast has made the leap.

TWO LOVE NOTES FOR YOUR PILLOW

1 *Sunset*

I did not look, you gave it to me —
that sight of your freckled breasts:
bats flown in the shaded green cave
of your dress, welling up to the light,
forming in my mind, the child I would
nestle there; in love, for love's sake ...

2 *Sunrise*

The Cyclops dawn studies with one
engorging eye, the eaten man;
the chewed-up, spat out soul that pens
a meaning to his life by night,
and sleepless crawls to morning's light
with hopes of art in tired bones.

ABROAD

Travelling through the World produces
a marvellous clarity in the judgement of men.

—Montaigne

I hate being abroad, generally speaking:
the further one gets from home the greater the misery.

—Philip Larkin

for
Imogen & Greta

SALUTATIO BEATRICIS

i

From the back
you are a rush of quick legs
open coat and clopping heels
striking noisily
down the walled flag-stone path
that slopes erratically
to the sea ...

ii

The wind has flung tentacles
of russet hair into the surge.
You do not turn, but twist
into a labyrinth of streets.

iii

It begins to rain. The cool
sweet scent has cast its net,
and I follow her echoes
with my tracing steps ...

ITALIAN OBSERVATION

Out of the old Italian fountain head —
out of the lion's mouth, this aqua vitae.
The champagne in your mouth dribbles.
You whisper to the man across the table.
He strokes your chin. The water chuckles.

Later, above the square, through the open
balcony window, across the bed where
you are winnowing the first harvest of sex:
the sound of the fountain. Had I spoken,
I'm sure it would have been so different.

HOMAGE TO FEDERICO FELLINI

Inizio

Through the peep-hole, a dull constellation
of candles, velvets, damasks, and the reflection
of mirrors *in camera*: the fine rococo walls
and gilded putti sparkle, and before the fire
the denuded nun and Casanova, half shaped,
are in animation: their flickering contours
merging to one: while secluded, the solitary
eye and hand are moving. This is Venice and
you are transported to the innocence of sin.

Mezzo

At Cinecittà, a lagoon of black plastic waves
rides a gondola to the Devil's eruption: that
welcoming blush of hot Carnevale — its melee
of dress; white masks, bright torches, cold
breath goosing voluptuous breasts; where
Harlequin and Pantaloon swive shy Columbine
(and Shepherdess): the cacophonous tunes and
cries for quarter, lost like a sob over facsimile
waters, and our cynical lovers perjure their flesh.

Fine

Lust's triumphal parade through bedroom
and ballroom: the beautiful show of *Priapus*
beating its ram into virginal pity — coaches
driven through snow — the long regretful
journey of withering ... Love, like clock-work
winding down, dancing its final minuet on thin
ice, jerky but coordinate, and perhaps we all
accept (after a life-time's searching) this last
amore; created for ourselves, inured to its cold.

ORTA SAN GIULIO — A TRIPTYCH

i

I have seen the graves. I have seen
the flat stones covering the dead
and lizards basking on their names,
warm and quiet in all this radiance
out of the blue. The only movement,
a cat washing in the marbled shade.

ii

On the cobbled path down from the *Sacro Monte*
a few pastel bank-side flowers ...
In front, and behind, the invisible footsteps.

iii

At night, every joke, curse, kiss
and foot-fall strikes the pink walls.

Wine bottles shatter in the narrow
alleys. The sounds, behaving badly,

riot in the Piazza and dance naked
on the deep black waters of the lake.

S. MARIE

La Vallée. The valley – this
Via Lactae; blessed, that cut-
away of blue dress, pointing
down, smart and sharp between

your breasts: the polished rounds
of common flesh I long to travel —
genuflect with kisses; caress to
unvarnished peaks, and express

all I feel from heart to finger-
tips — make all my sinful longings
a pilgrimage to this one holy place,
a fleshy trinity graced with peace ...

French Magdalena, the hands that
carved your sacred shape are
absolved of sin — for he knew
our hearts ... and love forgives.

Chinon, April 1990

A MODERN PISTOL SENDS A POSTCARD HOME

I sit, dangling my traveller's feet in the slow river.
Above, guarded by a couple of brisk nuns, a gaggle
of French school girls (white shirts, feral eyes,
bobby-socks, sandals of the brightest blue, an *élan*
of legs) scurry across the *Pont Vienne* at Chinon …

Beyond the worn river bank, bluebells and cuckoo
flowers have camped in a plantation of birchwood.
Birds chirp the *Qui va la?* of Harry *le Roi* and Pistol.
In my heart there is England: broken reflections,
as the *jeunes filles* pass — chattering — fast as canaries …

Wearily, I move on, down the dry road to Tours,
following that long ancestral march to Calais …
My heart lagging. The echo of belonging and urge
to possess, an unrequited load, heaped upon my back.

Chinon, April 1990

IN PARIS (*Un écho de EP*)

i

Cobble stones glacéd. The rain
has sweetened them: sugared
the mood in this Paris street —
the flood, smooth as silk ...

ii

Full gutters piss loudly down
slit-barred drains: fine melody
of a sombre kind; its wetness
connects with the low hung sky.

iii

Shop lights. The fast bloom
of tearful umbrellas. Under one,
still hidden, I predict her face —
lucid as an evening *fleur de lys* ...

LAURETTE WITH A COFFEE CUP

Henri Matisse, 1917

Laurette, your coffee has gone cold
and your pose (in that frosty white
chemise) too fixed. On a red ground,
the flesh (between stocking top and
hem) would have given off more heat —
but you are frigid, shaped by a brush
that's dipped in ice. Colours struck.
This mid-life Matisse is weary, and his
white-washed luxe, a shroud for youth.

IN PÈRE LACHAISE

In Père Lachaise
the monuments
to greatness are humbled
by this single rose

laid by a living heart
upon cold stone
or gangrened bronze:

effigy and monolith
crushed by bird song,
trees, and shadows;

and the fleeting time
we have for love,
sanguine, among these
memento mori ...

THE MAGDEBURG MAIDENS

Stone, maidens we presume, standing confused,
with stone maidenheads intact, caressed smooth
by mason's hands who loved them as daughters.

High, on the cathedral front at Magdeburg,
their plaits and little bosoms are fixed,
unable to ripen and balance round hips
that will never bear the weight of love.

At my stare, they each affect a smile,
concerned that I should place their frozen
imago puella on so neat a pedestal.

Only one, with open eyes can read
my thoughts, know I think these girls
that animate such delicate wrists
should live, and hold this new Pygmalion.

ABROAD

Why would I not want to be with my books?
I smoke my pipe. The balcony is small.
There is a chill in the air. The lake has
gone dark, and the mountains, mauve.

The sky is full of Valkyric clouds, slashing
at the waters and reflecting these thoughts,
drifting, to the Valhalla of home and hearth.

I am disconnected abroad. There is always
that vulnerable curiosity: an unnatural desire
to explore lake-sides, old alleys — the more
out-of-the-way vistas ... Then, there are also

the fleeting women: those Lorelei that call
to be followed into a phantom romance —
that 'what-might-have-been' we can safely

eroticise at home. Wing me back, Odin's
Maidens, to where my books, bed, and
guiding stars are all familiar ... Save me,
from this exile I've brought upon my self.

TO A CATALAN GRAND-DAUGHTER

for Greta

Flamenco
is an ampersand

driven mad

tappity-tap
stomp stomp

shooting the ground

the vibrant body
flashing and turning

rotació

its defiant sex
the unconquerable

female
ánima

rhythmically
en flames

ARGONAUTS

Beyond the Clashing Rocks, the secret
sea of delicate blue waves and endless
sun ... What shall we place upon it?

The Argo: oars dipping, backs bending
to every stroke — sweat, beards, a coarse
ripple of muscles ... buttocks clenching,

and the phallo-centric thoughts of Heroes
raised to a clearly spoken love ... On they
go — no ship of fools, foundered by Death
or woman's lust.

SAPPHIC FRAGMENT

Out of the hands of lamenting girls;
amid lachrymal song and funerary lamp-light,
the gift of a leather dildo from Alcaeus
made her laugh. The last joke;
the last attempt to deny her death —
the drunk's reasoning
that such coarseness would fire up
a rude health and restore her to his bed
of soft furs and white Egyptian linen.

LEATHER

Leather creaks. The flexions of Empire —
a masculine sound: the subtle animation
of sweat-softened breast plate — sand blown
or frost hardened, steaming with bloody exercise ...

Of saddle, sword-belt and marching sandal ...
And the whip ... It is the echo of Man's power:
hide-bound in codex, polished bright by many hands.

AFTER LI PO

Somewhere,
there is a jungle flower of great size
to place behind her ear

and after we have loved,
there's only the swaying bamboo
and rain

and that hobbled little shape,
holding her skirts — disappearing down
the mud-filled lane ...

AFTER DU FU

the sun
in trees
eastward

the sun
in clouds
westward

this day's
length
measured:

death,
the last
of one ...

FROM A SCRAP OF CINE FILM 1966

Sea urchins,
broken on the distant white reef
have spread
their dangerous spikes and shells
all over the fine white sands,
at Twiga beach,
below Mombasa.

The old 8mm film of me,
treading carefully
to the clear green sea,
fills me with a longing —
not for youth,
(or a less jerky photography)
but for Africa, herself.

INDULGENCES

By recollecting the pleasures I have had formerly, I renew them,
I enjoy them a second time, while I laugh at the remembrance of troubles
now past, which I no longer feel. A member of this great universe,
I speak to the air ...

—Giacomo Casanova

THE SIXTIES THING

for Brian Patten

Scene One (Profane)

The lamps are covered with red silk
so it's *Hell* in here and the tart I brought
is drunk. A simple strobe; fag smoke drifting
and the *Stones* beating the *Beach Boys* to a pulp.
Now, astride the joss-stick, she scents her cunt:
a Mogul trick; but tonight, before sin commingles
with diverse pox, she'll fuck us all, and we, her
lovers, forget the girl, but not the porous stink
of *Gordon's Gin*, and pricks glazed with yoni.

Scene Two (Sacred)

I sit in the college quad and catch sight of a
blue velvet skirt shimmering in sunlight; her
bird's nest of black hair tumbling over a cheese-
cloth top: brown nipples in obscura: green eyes:
lips puckered up in a thoughtful smirk — *Oh*, first
love, and all those songs about *Cecilia* and *Suzanne.*
I am caught: and summer, autumn and spring
dote on her shape and liberal chat, that we know
will lead to babies turning into ourselves again ...

ALUMNI

Down the telephone,
that familiar voice
(still honey and chocolate)
questioning my motives —
but I suppress this frisson
and make the usual congrats
re. new husband, daughter, job —
thinking it fortunate you took
the safer road, secure, and now
better off, to the middle class —
while I dropped, incrementally
to a caste more un-washed
and poetic. So here we are —
two dour cities distant; two
decades since the quad and
cloister — and that *Brideshead*
summer we broke apart, post
(or ante) graduation. You talk
more easily now; trying, in your
older heart, to be a friend ...

JAM MAKING

'Afterwards, when both were wives
*with children of their own...'**

All along the window sill, the ripening plums
she has placed so carefully with a tender hand:
two lines of fruity *glans*: an unconscious ranking
of her lovers' parts she has counted out for jam —
an aproned *Laura*, murdering songs from those
Goblin years, nervously, as she sweetens her pan;
forgiving, with every turn of the wooden spoon,
her priapic youth, when fruitful moisture ran.

Much and many the nights warm and dew pearly
She sought the wasting joys of juice and honey....

She would confess: *Fake* virginity, *Mock* love,
the *Dissembled* passions of her marriage bed —
to Daughters ... but *not* the clutching pleasure
Sisters take in latent thoughts of wicked men.

* *'Goblin Market' by Christina Rossetti*

FLIRTING

for Sabina Muller

'Flirting'. *Zu Flirten?* Flir-ting. The word
left to echo in the half-drunk wine-glass.

Now she is gone, everything seems part-
done, part said. I have an incomplete

sense of her body. The defining sex-signs
ignored in favour of watching her face.

The lips moving. The eyes sparkling in
lamp-light. Words (the fluid intimacy

of ideas) out-running the usual beasts.
The Tuscan red (more than the walk to

the station) flushing her cheeks. On the
bare platform those clumsy, mimed, un-

binding gestures: our parting, cheerfully
subdued. Only the Lindt cherry *chocolat*

délicieux (two gone from that sensual box)
denouement of my return to the empty house.

IMAGINE

Imagine a single dry-leafed oak standing
tall and mature in a pasture of sun-dried
grasses. It is August, and two lovers stretch
their naked bodies beneath its broad limbs.
(The tree has seen much and creaks in
satisfaction). Imagine this public nakedness
at dawn: the reluctance to dress; the many
halts to caress this or that intimate treasure
hidden before by night and shy measure ...
Imagine this love at first sight: this miracle
of a day and a night and a new day sent with
eye-conceiving lust. *Now*, imagine raw truths,
revealed to the light, in this transient Eden.

THE ISLAND

On the island there was only sunshine
and warmth and cliff walks, and the sea —
of course — all around, if you climbed to
the highest point of this insular place ...

A white-washed house, built of stone —
slate topped and tar-proofed — and about,
a flower garden of modest size, with lawn
sloped for exotic trees and all enclosed

from the wildest wind. Here was my solitude:
my time to write — my thoughtful pipe always
full and lit: food and women conjured up
when appetite grew, or I needed something

more ... without Prospero's power to trans-
mute a page of dreams into solid life, this self-
delusion comes more frequently now: madness
bled out, in a flow of insubstantial words ...

DREAM, AFTER THE TEMPEST

I was chasing Miranda through her father's
cornfield ... Fuck the logs and fardel bearing.
Fuck the Magician's warning and my promise
to leave *intactus* his little daughter's virgin-knot.

The sun has turned flesh and sky white.
Youth burns in the bristling mass of seed heads.
I will put my weight upon her — go inside
her quenching place ... She is glorious:

like the Venus of Botticelli brought to life —
crucified by me on this stony earth ...
Here are the words that do violence to art —
a fantasy made real, when it's blown apart.

JASMINE

There is nothing like the scent of jasmine.
It is the carved saints in lonely churches;
the voices of lost women; the sun of youth;
the hill-path between low hedges; a first
love never forgotten; the flesh in moonlight
that turned towards us; it is death; the pallid
flower; the constellations of remembering.

MR WORMWOOD GOES TO CHURCH

I did not believe the Old French saying;
'Girls that squirm in church have soft bottoms'.
But at Mass, she moved from side to side,
subtly, and only from behind would I have
noticed the drop-pearl earrings sway —
the blond plait flick ... Of course, it could
have been a *Greater Sin* that shifted her,
or prick of medieval splinter, sharp nail,
some foul itch? But I can only think of
white haunches, pillowed on wood, and how
when the service *Endeth* — I may commend
Faith, Sermon — the Grace of God — and with
the Devil's aid, pursue that course of Love
that will prove (or disprove) the Gallic wit.

ANNE'S COTTAGE, BISHOPS CANNINGS

I took possession of the cottage in my heart:
yet it was wrong to think old walls and thatch
could cure all ills: dream, the cosy rooms a place
to cheer myself and settle with old books,
a nagging cat, and friends, sequentially,
all sharing the chatty arm-chaired hearth ...

Or in Summer, be at rest in its sun-filled garden,
set beside the seductive lane — that easy walk;
a pilgrim-path to pub and prayer ... It was love:
covetous love — the tragic state of mind where
more is lost than found. I gave it up. But think,
never again, will I find a place to love so much ...

THE WIDOW & MR WORMWOOD

The sexy black dress she wears is chic, hitting
just the right stylistic note as a counterpoint
to grief. The sun stabs light through the stained
glass windows: it ignites her hair into a burning
bush, licking her back to an alluring shape …
On both sides, a child cradles her hips: a neat
triptych, standing the strain of hymns and mawkish
valedictions to their dear departed stiff …

She is young, and will make good the time she's
lost to an uncomfortable neglect. The last seeds
have died within her: the stains that marked her
sheets are washed away. A green season will
succeed the crepèd wreath. I will comfort the
empty widow. But first: to the happy grave …

THE ROMEO Y JULIETA CIGAR

The huge *Romeo y Julieta* cigar —
nostrils sniffing: the scent of the
sweaty Cuban girl's silken thigh
a residual on the dust-dry phallus
Freud constantly denied symbolic ...

I wet its tip. If this is mock fellatio,
then *I get it* girls and guys, but light,
and draw the musky vapour in, sharp
as wine, un-quenching; mellow to the
fatalistic mind — the cumulus exhale

curling and uncurling: Hamlet's joke
of clouds, fading to wraiths ... Critic,
leave me this reverie of smoke, burning
through dreams; entangling thoughts ...

PAGAN

I need to sacrifice a virgin
to enflame my libido

but at seventy,
consecrated nuns

and other left-overs
are un-hardening choices

and being morally predisposed
to what is kind and legal

my ego considers
those aspects of *quantum-time*

vis a vis past realities
(theoretically un-erasable)

where my virility
still kindles new life,

ecstasy, and the deluded
'*Present*' that never dies …

AN APOLOGY TO WOMEN

for Mike Hogan

Woman — *the collective whole* — I've not handled
you well; for only the painter's art or camera lens
can catch the full scope of your perfection.

Words are not enough: and as a man, it would
be wrong to judge your sex by outward form alone.
But the curves that define your body; from *ovum*

to *breasts; hips, buttocks, belly, nape of neck*; *eyes*
of many colours; *lips* that are so soft and red;
skin that reflects alabaster, ebony or bronze:

the *arms*, falling with grace to gentle *hands*;
the wet *)o(* between your *legs*, I still nakedly
worship — and confess my sin to God — who

forgives; smiling wryly at the fallen man, still
enthralled, since Eden, to an ever-changing Eve.

MISS STICKNEY'S POEM

Written at the Rimbaud Unit, Akaroa Clinic,
New Zealand, Pacific Province, Earth (Sol 3)
6 August, 2154

The very meaninglessness of life forces man to create his own meaning.

—Stanley Kubrick

for

Lawrence

DISK I

'Miss Stickney must be proud of her two moons,' I said
as I put down my glass on the window ledge
to take in the panoramic views of Tharsis
and jaundiced clouds fingering Olympus ...

She was confused. I explained how Mrs. Hall
(née Stickney) had persuaded husband Aspha
to look again, to strain his eyes to find the moons
we see each night, fall and rise in brilliance —

'Oh,' she said. A disinterested tone, yet
meaning more. She was agitating for bed.
I heard her get up from the soft-lounger and pad
half-naked to some space uncomfortably near ...

 ... Outside dusk is falling and the familiar stars
rise up from the deep blue sunset ... Mandelstam
was right — salt on black velvet — salt in a wound ...
We've had our first birth — only death pauses ...

She breathes lightly behind me — seems aroused.
I sense her tension. We are not the match we thought.
If home is where the heart is, low down, by the horizon,
Earth is setting — is it she I love? This madness

for green and blue — and a weightiness to being —
and falling in love? ... I acquiesce to the pressure
of her breasts on my back — am returned to my role
in the 'reproductive needs' of this ochre world.

DISK 2

Our son was born in a square room. Its lights blanching,
but grotesquely functional: Kubrick would have found
the scene film-worthy. Only the blood — furiously Martian
messed things up — agitating my loathing of red — until it

dried to a shitty brown, that eased the anger I can now hardly
contain ... The baby cries, flexing limbs with a native strength
short-time will make un-Martial and un-Carteresque: his
childhood paced out in lighter steps.

And memories? Our enchanted isle has no reveries of past.
There is a frost tonight, as every night — but he is warm:
the temperature perfect and automatic — so no blue flame
for me to note — and no prospect of an unexpected caller.

DISK 3

We holiday *en famille* in Marsport, Arcadia. Trees: flowing
water; retail pods — screens with vid-plays cast from Earth.
Meetings over lunch with other perfect couples — breeding
pairs, despite the red loathing I see clouding their eyes ...

'Anyone read Casanova, Stendhal, De Sade?' An illiterate
silence is remoulded into the required verbal etiquette.
The Psychos are probably concerned — I saw the cameras
triangulate. I shall get *the* call. This will be my umpteenth

confession of desires; for wantonness, drunkenness,
gluttony— name your Deadly Sin. For I want it; disorder
and love. The sands are always shifting here — under minds
and feet. My son smiles and farts a partial change of air.

Your mother is looking suicide pills. There is a partial
vacuum. I am drawn in again to what I have become,
neither Arean nor Earthling, but something fractured
and in-between.

DISK 4

I ride the tube to the Gardens of Hellas — past solar farms
sparking shards of light — their snug order, partly obscured
by sprites of sand — tall vortices in a bland desolation —
almost alive ... I long for green sward ...

We pull in with the kind of *hiss* I remember from old films.
Night; the concertina doors of a bus opening suddenly ...
A bee passes my ear as I vacate the carriage. Unexpected
in a carbon-fibre station — the dark hub centering π^2 km

of fertile diversity, all enclosed in sky-high domes,
clouded (like back home) — but bottled up; un-wandering
over orchards, fields, and patches of more exotic fare,
tended, and intended, to keep us healthy ... and sane.

I breath earth. I breathe *my* Earth. The globus of home
sickness is rising again as I move to greet the farming team.
I shall assess production, but playing in my mind, the faded
archives of village green and harvest fair — like in old films,

or films of books we've lost: Tess and Bathsheba, even in
our colonial gear, could be Hardyesque. These women have
all the beauty of labour, but are unnaturally placed — gene-
picked for fertility and omnivorous for passion, they offer

only a denuded love ... Caleb Line's advice to Dominick
(a vid-hero from long ago) rings true: 'If you want to study
people, watch old films ...' I must prime the play to view
again ... The story of a man, out of Time ...

Back home, under the IR clean-up beam, her battered body
is slightly cooked. I will confess — freedom with an ironic
locking up. The red mist no metaphor. My mind has turned.
Thoughts hobble down bloody corridors, completely lost ...

DISK 5

I don't recall the launch:
only the bruised orange ball hanging in the window,
and I, floating around, not gravitating to any place
in this nice safe room.

The Ai nurse has pulsed another dose —
of drugs, smells, and a Corelli concerto I've always loved;
and yet — I hum *Singin' in the Rain*: (thump thump) —
I must sing in the rain ...

DISK 6

It's good here at the Akaroa Clinic.
I've written a therapeutic poem … I can see the Canterbury
Bight and South Pacific … I'm gonna wash that man …
Happy happy talk … I have written a poem. It begins:

'Miss Stickney must be proud of her two moons,' I said
as I put down my glass on the window ledge.
That's when I thought, that's when I thought,
'I must write a poem, or go mad.' It will begin:

'Miss Stickney must be proud of her two moons,' I said
as I put down my glass on the window ledge
to take in the panoramic views of Tharsis
and jaundiced clouds fingering Olympus …

VOYAGING OUT

*One glance at a book and you hear the voice of another person,
perhaps someone dead for a thousand years.
To read is to voyage through time.*

Cherish the pale blue dot, the only home we've ever known.

—Carl Sagan

i.m.

Sir Patrick Moore

VOYAGING OUT

Voyaging through the stars again tonight,
my eyes telescope the void to places far
removed from this mess we call The Earth:
the burial ground; the once all-providing
mother, teacher, nurse we've pimped to
destitution. Which is why I long to leave:
have my roots shaken out and planted a-
new, light-years distant … A foolish hope,
for a man, time-trapped; scrawling words
in the ancient way — their strange pattern,
the one iota of *Self* that might spindrift to
the Tantalus of stars, forever out of reach …

ECCE HOMO

1

The poem tasted of sour wine.
He spat it out: slammed doors:
threw books — imagined a fire
that would burn the whole
cursed effort of putting life
(as he saw it) into words ...

2

Long before dawn, he lay
in the garden. At his back
Mother Earth, and above;
the unreachable spill
of the *Via Lactae* — its milk,
richer than any human love.

3

Behold the Man, spinning
in the dark: the light of
the past *netted* in his *not*
unique mind — its outward
start, falling back into the
deeper spaces of himself.

IN THE OBSERVATORY

Before dawn, in the mist, filtering through
trees and over grass, the bird song. I listen
while my chilled eye wanders star field
after star field, until I fix on one I cannot
name, knowing it is home to some other
night-loving soul, voyaging out ... I can
feel the empathy; the unreachable bond.
In this pause, I describe the here and now:
do you comprehend this solitary echoing?

MARS TRIP

for Sir Patrick Moore at Eighty

Speed, denied the sensual grip of wind
and ocean, unbucked by waves, straight
as an arrow, the ship's tip, aimed at *Ares*
leaves only a wake of Euclidian lines.

The smell of honeysuckle. From this little
plastic phial, a June evening tries to deny
the existence of steel bulkheads and
sterile air. He floats, eyes closed, within
the chrysalis of hope: the stars are steady;
the remote Earth a crackle of insect static.

Day-dreams come more frequently now:
the unrequited love of green and blue —
his arms embrace an entire world.
Homer's poem enchants from disk:
the fibril siren-song on every sense
that seeks the touch of home and love.

Bound safely in his memories, he makes
the long return to an old beginning.
No hubris strides his brave new world;
he knows his place, and stands in awe
of the journey made, Odysseus-like.

A MARTIAN LOOKS IN

a great calm

the wind
shifting

waves of sand

the sun beats down
there's nothing

just sand

and a few bones
and broken artefacts

junked on a planet

that failed
to make amends

s/f koan

This denizen
of the Red Planet

this mutated
creature

tall
and frail boned

in silk toga
among

the capitols
and columns

of this
New Rome

looks
to the pale twilight

and sees
the old home

an iota
of fractured blue.

RESURRECTION

(With thanks to Reanimation Program D54316:
Patent No.4004/2228CE – The Ego Institute.)

Recreate me. Come on.
Dig — me — up ...
The DNA chain,
un-chained, reformed,
re-animated
by this metal brain's
fine electronic flow ...

By this mimicry
I grow, bit by bit,
until I am whole again,
and come to love myself
with all the old strength,
unblemished by this
timeless conversion ...

Now
no longer awed by infinity
I embrace the stars
and, immortal,
out-pace God — vaulting,
with greater strides,
this old diminished universe.

YOU & I

Out among the stars
say my name ...

I shall hear, and reply
in echoes of my voice.

Yet my true self,
however read,
speaks unchanged

to the present *You*
from the phantom *I.*

THE

REVELATION

OF

THE

ESOTERIC

MESSIAH

He had followed the call of space. He sang and he listened ...

[Sonnet to Orpheus I XX]

Oh, and there's Night, there's Night, when the wind full of cosmic space
Feeds on our faces: for whom would she not remain, longed for,
Mild disenchantress, painfully there for the lonely heart to achieve?

[First Duino Elegy]

—Rainer Maria Rilke

for
my Mother

THE JOURNEY

The shadow of the bird has marked the wall,
blackened my face, drawn the eyes of the stranger
ever closer, and I am afraid, for the dark is behind
and the red wave of evening is crashing down.
The darkness has come to claim the turning away;
the turning half of all I am, and ever will be:
this blue O; the world stage from which we fly
and dip a toe in star-light. The roar of flight;
the rush of distance come, dashing over the edge
of time. The face of God is masked in shame.
We outstride our Maker, and have arrived —
never the same again ...

THE ARRIVAL

Our craft has found your beauty.
A sperm to ovum. The opiate-aired curve
we ride to. Invade its virgin mist,
and twist to land … There are met
by a white star's rising and a dewed green
that wets bare feet.

As we alight — the smaller step is hers.
Mine is a great leap that takes me nowhere.
There is a moon under which something pulls
like a spider's web, or the slackened strings
of the Aeolian harp

like plain-song in empty space. The first night
we are Adam and Eve, and with the first light
I awake to find a monster, or wiser being,
has taken the guts of my sleeping friend.
I recall her last words: 'This is going to be fun …'
and cast what I loved into our quantum fire.

THE LAMENTATION

The rain outside is making the grass greener,
and the pale cheeks of remembered friends
a delusion, when choosing raindrops, or tears
as the most eloquent metaphor for grief.
She is our first dead: the queen and mother
of this new world; the un-leaven saviour
of our cynical faith ...

Alone again, the Vitruvian man does somersaults
like a harlequin; his mad hands and feet grasping
at their full extent, the limits, the very edge ...
So she went into Heaven —
that is all we comprehend;
the figures do not add up;
the theories are always flawed
and God still laughs behind the proscenium arch.

THE CONCEPTION

Wakefulness has outlasted the dark,
and alone there is a strange completeness
broken by an unexplained sound —
the hellish Lark, absurd in size, hovering
in a mauve mist over trees surreal in softness
and shape — a children's book, eroticised —
a naked angel, flapping its wings; the body —
our nightmare's vulgar hope; the succubus
of dreams shaped into beauty ...

I cannot resist this grotesque love;
and am transformed by a lust song-bound
to flesh; the merging of parts, unparallel
and bestial ... I assume this is the helical
constant — the universal — but am beyond
logic or reason: there has been
a consecration of new life ...

REVELATION: THE NEW MESSIAH

Your breasts were the memory
of fallen rose-petals; faint pink flowers
that have died, never to rise again.
This is the curse of our union —
the cold angel's egg that has broken
and spread exquisite wings across the sky;
the fledged hybrid of deception:
God's new toy.

She is the Messiah of new worlds:
the anointed Being, mysterious and universal —
to the end of the continuum — birthing
again and again the reality
we pretend to understand —
the great and terrible Mother,
feeding love through the stars ...
And in this suckling, we are beguiled.

Author's Note on 'The Revelation of the Esoteric Messiah'

The five sections of this poem offer a future myth set in a time when humanity has voyaged out into a boundless universe. The journey to an alien world instigates a new beginning — a reset. Here, the original 'primitive' human instinct to revere the mysterious fecundity of all nature in the form of The Great Mother proves to be well founded. Events unfold on this new world culminating in a metamorphosis that anoints and reveals a new Messiah – the deliverer – God's agent to restore the essential feminine nature of all existence. This poem challenges the patriarchal masculinity of both Angels and Supreme Beings as proclaimed by Rilke and Nietzsche.

Mankind's hubris is revealed in The Journey. We go beyond the human dramas enacted at Shakespeare's simple 'Wooden O' and out from the turning 'blue O' of our home planet to beyond all God-given limits. The Arrival of this new Adam and Eve in an alien Eden predictably starts with the man assuming dominance: his 'great leap' compared to her 'smaller step'. But there is a moon; the planet of Aphrodite and Diana the huntress. This feminine force destroys the image of the 'lesser' female and the man is forced to cast his idealization of the female into a dissolving fusion with the elemental universe.

The man alone gives up hope. The Lamentation is for all the things he had expected from the 'mother of this new world'. He enacts a dumb show of frustration because his scientific certainty rejects God the Creator. From this madness he enters into a mystical state and is awakened spiritually by the song of a surreal Lark; the enlightener of dramatic lovers. He cannot resist this transforming creature which temporarily displays itself as a beautiful angel. He is seduced by his own lustfulness and mates with her, resulting in The Conception of the new Messiah.

The Revelation is that of the new saviour, born into and becoming all creation. The Great Mother, restored to nurture the Universe and once again 'feed love through the stars'.

HOMAGE

TO

THE

CORPSE

OF

MARCEL

DUCHAMP

Besides, it's always the others who die

—Marcel Duchamp

Black on White

Conceptualize
the
Meaning

Expect Words

Black Shapes
White Universe

Follow Me

Black
on
White

Now
I have You

You Can Have

●

Moving
on
White

The
Aerial Shot
Beloved
of
Birds

Pecking Out
the
Black Eyes
of
the
Hanging Corpse

Black
or
White

Always
Black
in
the
After-Life
Party
Death Throws
for
The Chosen

The Wheel of Life
Doesn't Work

Too Animate
Too
Shot Through
With Movement

Like Glass That Breaks
or
The Peep Show
You Hid

The Last Voyeur
of
Lust

Do Not Think

L'Origine du Monde

or

The Light of the World

So

There
is
Black and White

White Stars
Black Space

Held
Together
in
One Universe

But I Lie

It's
Too
Simple

Black
and
White

No Mention
of
GOD
or
the
DEVIL

Bound in the Helix

That
is
Invisible

But

Turns in the Mind
that
Loves Insanity
and
Tries to Mend

Make a Unity
of
Black and White

As I Have
Here
Written

Seen
Through
Art-Less

R. Mutt

Eyes

You

Thinking

BODIES

For in the particular acts of human life,
it is not the interior soul and the true man,
but the exterior shadow of the man alone,
which laments and weeps ...

—Plotinus

BODIES

Even if he rises with the lark,
its song is dead in those benighted eyes.

He is a man of the twilight woods:
a man to embrace the dying warmth

settling in his arms — the chilled flesh
grave in Autumn — the buried love ...

He that entombs bodies thus, regrets
and would swing at the appointed time,

but day-by-day reprieves the curse
of knowing what he's done ...

LUCIEN PISSARRO:

The Day After – 30 July 1890

Now Dr. Gachet weeps, grieved
but sly, and above the sloped fields
rooks swoop and upward moan
over this land of growing wheat
where an artist's blood still lies.

The sun is yellow; the blue haze
speckled, where dark wings rise.

Despair is a Brotherhood —
and while I write, I am carried up.

Despair is a Brotherhood —
where one dies — but another says,
I live — struggling to fly unbound,
protesting, *Oh for more days like these
where the harvest sun is bright ...*

'IT COMES, IT COMES'*

The flesh gives out. It must. Skin
giving way to blanched bones.
The private grin of the corpse
in its box, as it settles to dissolution,
resolving to a perfect form, in the ennui
of the grave, or honour of the tomb.

We all ignore Mercutio — embarrassed
by the Reaper cutting too soon —
the seasons, moving on, to our own
ripening — remembering the one thing
not lived through, but imagining *it*
in every form, as it rattles by

industrious in its swing of blade —
every time, scything closer; the blackness
nearer — the *null* place ... *It comes*, it comes
in chilled limbs and failing breath — or
as the shock and pain of an assassin's blade:
it comes; *darker* than we realised.

*The last words of John Keats, 1821

HANGED BY THE NECK

i.m. Edith Thompson (1893-1923) *

Sat down in a faint, she was away —
the broken neck, the gentle sway of limbs
limp above the fallen chair,

the blood, the child, the womb —
all fallen, all laid bare below the beam
that chains the rope that creaks

with the pulsing swing of a girl on air —
pendulum of dead flesh, once animate,
once a fire of sex —

her delicate little shoes awash with waste,
pointing down to the bloody floor:
the Law's abattoir, bathed in winter sun;

and through a muffled silence comes
the hangman's pardon:
God ... What have I done?

Edith Thompson was executed on 9 January 1923 at Holloway Prison, London. She was condemned to death on the basis of 'Common Purpose' as a consequence of her lover, Freddie Bywaters, having stabbed her husband Percy Thompson in a jealous rage. Bywaters twice made confessions that he had acted alone, but she was still charged and condemned on the basis of circumstantial evidence. Effectively mad in the weeks before her execution, she was heavily sedated and unable to stand on the gallows — so was placed in a bosun's chair to be dropped. No one had examined her to see if she was pregnant. The drop caused an abortion. No post-mortem was carried out and files relating to the hanging are sealed for one hundred years. Her executioner, John Ellis — traumatized by what he had done — committed suicide.

ROOKS

Chapel Stile, Westmorland, 1982

Down the chimney,
tuned in soot,
the raucous cry of rooks,
chipping at grey slate;
tapping messages
from the heather-bled stones
of the fells —

roof-top heralds,
bringing
the cold landscape's call
for a mergence of mood
and oblivion of self.

'GEORGE' 1960–1980

F- M- Psychiatric Hospital, 1980

George was very quiet on the ward.
Sat and stared. No trouble — and Dad
came every moment he could spare.

But I could not spare George, or un-
wind with bare hands the looped wire
wrapped around his neck, or lift his

dead weight: get his blood to throb
under my fingers ... *Does God hear*
screams for help — or bless torn hands?

Later, taking Dad aside ... The bowed
heads and that palsied second death
creeping over the one who loved ...

For me, this death has lasted forty years.

IT'S ELECTRIFYIN'!

for Willie Francis*

When the electric hits that techno helm
and grieve, cracking the spine, arching
the back — the roasted calf steaming,
and the clenched jaw hidden behind
its leather flap — we witness ingenuity's
lightning: the pain endured from this
dull stingless hum, not cruel or unusual,
but the application of *Good Ol' Yankee
Know-how* — like fried chicken, or burgers
sizzling on a grid, served up for its public
good: Revenge, a savoury dish, delivered hot ...
A pre-Hellish burn, unlike the rope (that
old time pleaser), this, the *modern* way to
send those sinful brothers straight to God.

*There have been four thousand, four hundred and fourteen judicial executions by electric chair in the United States to date [2024]. The only known survivor was Willie Francis; a black Louisiana teenager, aged sixteen (condemned, unsurprisingly, by an all-white jury). The local sheriff said: 'This boy really got a shock when they turned that machine on...'[!] A year and a day later, on 9 May 1947, he was strapped back into 'Gruesome Gertie' and 'successfully' electrocuted.

MEMENTO MORI — A QUARTET

i

swan feathers in sharp reeds —
somewhere,
dark waters shroud a death

ii

in the copse, no sound
except the sniffing of the dog
and the anger of fallen elms

iii

this child's gravestone
such a little thing
hidden in tall grasses

iv

on this old sick bed
seeing you only in dreams
I fall with the rain

EARTH WORK

We do not know where death awaits us:
so let us wait for it everywhere. To practise death is to practise freedom.
A man who has learned how to die has unlearned how to be a slave.

—Michel de Montaigne

for

L. H. W. Bailey

EARTH WORK

My hands; into their fine lines
the dirt that stains, root deep —
almost suffusing the blood,
flowing into swollen blue veins
to the gnarled, knotty joints.

Yesterday; the white sun
burned my face — the esoteric
man — aching in all parts with
Adam's curse. Today, these
words, hard as any acre dug.

SPRING

Spring. Its cold air blowing away zephyric
gentleness: shattering rainbows; its heavy
grey clouds split by plump hills, shamelessly
flashing their sunny décolletage.

All this season's hopes abandoned as Ravens
gather on tombs; Magpies glut on raided eggs
and the helpless Wren flutters, piteously,
in a Cat's mouth. Spring. These longer days

with the Earth cut open, and the harvester's
bargain of *Life for Life* always masking
Death's silent laughter, as he scythes our time
and gleans each speck of nature's suffering.

STRANGE MEETING

Horse-trodden, its skin unsplit
and perfectly pressed in mud,
the recently dead field mouse
was now rigid with frost
when we came upon it
during our chilly
morning walk ...

We discussed — over its corpse —
the arrogance of riders;
their full weight and class;
and how fatal these
crescent hoof-marks
on this scantling art
of mouse-bones ...

CAT

for Clotilde

You wash so carefully the same place,
rough tongue smoothing the tangled fur,
teeth gnawing at burrs, but not observing,
as do I, the fine dust, cobwebs, and odd
small leaves, gathered on your coat —
the only remaindered clues, the only
dumb explanation of where you've been
since the last tryst in our on-going game
of love and evasion. How I have come
to appreciate this partly joined life:
my *muse* — my *familiar*: my *Mephisto* wife.

DETECTIVE STORY

The black rat, after stealing bird-seed
and chewing bulbs, has bored holes
through the compost heap — convoluted
routes to apple cores, broken eggs
and other choice foods.

My cat, like a detective, sniffs the base
of this rotting pile: the scent still strong;
the crime-scene still pungent with clues.
Tonight, while I hunt vermin with words,
her more natural talent will snap a neck.

FATHER

My father,
his old green cardigan
draped carelessly
over the spade's handle,
pauses,
feet astride the new-dug clay,
to unearth a fag-end
deep
in his work-worn pocket ...

A lighter clicks.
The brief flame
hallows his face,
gaudy,
in the deep blue twilight —
marking his place
in the scheme of things:
forever beloved,
and loving.

Haiku Coda

twilight
watching my father dig
one star above his head

LINES WRITTEN IN A WILTSHIRE CHURCHYARD

May beckons the past. All time surges in:
old memories, combining ... So it goes,
the month, doing (again) what it always does:
recalling life, and all the books I've ever read:

that panorama of personal and gestalt —
Everything, being associated with Now,
and back, further and further; the ancestors
rising through every age to possess me ...

I have to face it: I'm a dying end-point
that's moved little. Here, even these solid
chapters of mortality are fading — eternal
rain, frost and sun, grinding them away

above and below.... Love survives only
in the flesh. The baroque quip is true:
Thee who reads today tomorrow shall be bones.
Comforting, isn't it? Perhaps I need to sit,

quiet in the May sun, satisfied I've lived
so long, insensible to the surety of death;
watching the breathful skies scud along:
just a wordy Stranger, waiting his turn.

THE BOAT

I rowed over the glass lake in a mist
bellowed from the nose of some hidden beast, far off,
beyond the birds singing in the shadow tops of trees
edging the land — still out of reach.

Water chimed down the oars' edges.
A wake of vortices trod back:
rowlocks clumped with a poetic beat.
I would have been lost,
had not some sense of direction
(part historic; part ancestral self-myth)
familiar with voyaging beyond the certain,
guided my helm.

It's at times like these I know the Old Gods live,
and from their un-Christian paradise
the past blood still flows within my shriven quick:
the echo sounds to my deepest self —
marking the shallows of that Other-world
from which I drift ...

THE END

There, boxed up, not a breath or thought — not even
an echo in that segregated state re-defined as 'corpse'.

So this is how it ends: the draughty church; rain outside —
mourners spaced like pieces in a game (with one left out).

The few familiar hymns. A sob or two. Resonating words
summing up an already forgotten past. This is *The End*.

The *Quick* and *Dead* parade, re-group around the grave —
and down it goes, the human crate lost to sight. *Earth to*

earth. Place flowers. Walk away. The muted conversations;
their subscript: *Glad to be alive and see another day.*

Kevin Bailey
1991

ABOUT THE AUTHOR

Kevin Bailey was born within the bounds of the ancient Borough of Wallingford, Berkshire, in 1954. After spending part of his childhood in East Africa, he returned to England and attended Wallingford Grammar School. He was later educated at the University of York and Bath Spa University.

In 1990 he founded the international literary journal *HQ Poetry Magazine*, which he still edits and publishes independently. He has been closely involved in the activities of the London poetry group Piccadilly Poets and the Live Poets Society in Bath.

In 2000 he edited (with Lucien Stryk) the classic anthology *Contemporary Haiku*. Since 2001, he has assisted and judged at the annual *Poetry on the Lake* festival held at Orta San Giulio in Italy. In 2004, he adjudicated the prestigious *Sasakawa Prize for Haikai.* His poetry and commentaries have appeared in a wide range of publications. He is the author of five collections of poetry, and a translation of Sappho.

In recognition of his astronomical research he was elected a Fellow of the Royal Astronomical Society in 2013. He is also an Assistant Director (Uranus) of the Saturn, Uranus & Neptune Section of the British Astronomical Association.

At present he lives in Wiltshire, at the heart of his beloved North Wessex countryside with his feline amanuensis, Dorothy.

This collection excludes the author's *Collected Haiku*, published under the title *By The Way*, by the Red Moon Press in the United States in 2023, and the translations of sixty-four poems and fragments by Sappho, included as a separate section in the 2005 collection *Surviving Love* published by Bluechrome.